D0387502

Straight
from the
Heart
for MOM

Straight From the Heart
for Mom

by

Richard Exley

Tulsa, Oklahoma

Straight From the Heart for Mom
ISBN 1-56292-092-8
Copyright © 1995 by Richard Exley
P.O. Box 54744
Tulsa, Oklahoma 74155

Published by Honor Books
P.O. Box 55388
Tulsa, Oklahoma 74155

Presented to:

Moms

On the Occasion of:

A wounderful day with Moms.

Presented by:

The Mu Family

Date:

_13/7/98_

I Love you mom.
Christopher

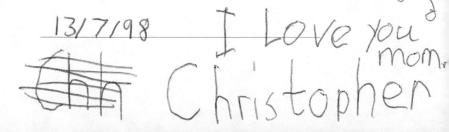

DEDICATION

To Irene Exley and
Hildegarde Wallace,
mothers extraordinary.

Contents

CHAPTER

1

A Mother's Love

"*Once you thought that love was always warm and wonderful, now you know different. Sometimes a mother's love is painful beyond words.*"

Chapter 1

ᖗ

A Mother's Love

You stand in the doorway gazing wistfully at your daughter who is nearing sleep. Her caramel-colored hair is spread out on the pillow like a halo, and she seems especial pretty in the glow of the night light. As you stare in near hypnotic fascination, your heart heavy with love, you find yourself reminiscing, reliving your short life together.

Was there ever a time when you didn't love her? You think not. Even before she was conceived, you remember feeling this love. At the time you didn't identify it for what it was, but it was there, yearning for expression, longing for the moment when the object of its devotion would appear. Clearly you recall the first hints of morning sickness and the excitement of watching the home pregnancy test stick change colors. In that moment, although she was only a microscopic zygote, you knew that your love had found its object.

Now your "baby" is five years old, and tomorrow she will attend her first day of kindergarten. For a moment, bittersweet tears blur your vision, but with a determined effort you blink them away. You won't think about tomorrow, not yet. Instead, you relive the day of her birth.

The travail of labor is just a dim memory, but the miracle of her birth is as vivid now as it was that spring afternoon five years ago. When the doctor placed her in your arms for the first time, you remember thinking that your heart would burst. Never could you have imagined that it was possible to love anyone as much as you loved her. And you were sure you would never love her more than you did in that moment.

With unspeakable joy, you counted her fingers and toes, just as your mother had counted yours. You held her close to your breast and poured out your love in nonsense syllables. Although you knew she could not understand a word you were saying, you never doubted her ability to comprehend the love you showered upon her.

But you were wrong. Not about her ability to comprehend your love, but about never loving her more. You have always loved her completely, but over the years your capacity to love has grown; consequently, your love for her is greater now. You have always loved her with all your heart, but now your heart is bigger.

Once you thought that love was always warm and wonderful, now you know different. Sometimes a mother's love is painful beyond words.

Like the time she wandered off while you were carrying in the groceries. When you stepped into the front yard to call her, she was nowhere to be seen. Half a block away, high school hot-rodders were burning up the street, and you experienced a moment of paralyzing panic as you imagined her crushed beneath their screaming tires. Breathing a desperate prayer, you rushed toward the corner, frantically calling her name.

At the tender age of three, when her soft skin and big eyes made her seem especially vulnerable, she came down with strep throat, and her temperature spiked at a hundred and four degrees. It was a torturous time for both of you. She could hardly swallow, and her ragged wheezing tore at your heart. From the dim shadows of her sick room, death seemed to leer at you, and in spite of the doctor's assurances you found yourself fearing for her life. Try as you might, you could not escape your tormenting thoughts. Desperately, you prayed, begging God to spare her, telling Him that there was absolutely no way you could live without her. In moments like that, a mother's love is an open wound.

Mostly though, your love is joyously poignant, and now your memories are kaleidoscopic, leapfrogging from scene to scene. You remember the day of her christening, the first time she said "Mommy," her first birthday and her early stumbling steps. They wash over you now, bringing with them a fresh realization of how much you love this sleeping child, more than you have ever loved her before.

You should let her sleep, tomorrow is a big day, but you cannot help yourself. Kneeling beside her bed, you bury your face in her hair and whisper your love into its fragrant softness. Half awake, she senses your presence and puts her arms around your neck, pulling your head hard against the side of her face. The embrace only lasts for a moment, then sleep reclaims her, and her arms grow limp. Carefully, you tuck the covers around her before planting a soft kiss on her forehead.

In the doorway, you glance back a final time. How desperately you wish that she could know the depth of your love. You cannot tell her, try as you might, for there are no words to express what you feel. Even if there were, and if she could somehow comprehend their meaning, the totality of your love would still escape her. Softly, you whisper, "Good night, my little one."

Tiptoeing down the hall, you comfort yourself with the knowledge that someday she will understand how you feel. Someday when she becomes a mother and has a child of her own.

CHAPTER

2

School Days

"With frightening clarity you realize that a chapter in your life is closing. For him it is a beginning, a new adventure, the first step in a journey that will eventually take him into adulthood, away from you, and into a life of his own."

Chapter 2

∽

School Days

You stand on the porch and wave good-bye, blinking hard to hold back the tears. The family car, bearing its precious cargo, backs out of the driveway and heads down the street. After a moment's hesitation, you hurry to the curb and watch until it turns the corner and disappears. Slowly, you trudge back up the driveway and into the house, silent now in its emptiness.

How can this be? you ask yourself for the hundredth time. It seems it was only yesterday that you were bringing him home from the hospital for the very first time. Before you knew it, he was crawling and into everything. He wasn't a bad baby, just active! Then came the terrible twos, and you had your moments. Moments when you were exhausted and at your wits' end. Moments when you wished and dreamed for the day he would be old enough to begin school. Now you experience more than a twinge of guilt at the memory of such feelings. How could you have been so blind, you wonder, to the brevity of his preschool years?

Once, when you were especially stressed out, your mother tried to encourage you. "Enjoy these days," she said. "Before you know it, he'll be grown and gone." Wearily, you brushed a strand of hair back from your face, took a deep breath and then returned to the milk spill you were cleaning up. The look you gave your mother said it all. School days couldn't come soon enough for you.

How nearsighted your thinking now seems, on this his first day of kindergarten. Biting your lip, you brush a tear from your cheek and run through a mental checklist in an effort to appease your inordinate concern. He'll be fine, you tell yourself, but you feel no better. Belatedly, you realize that it's not him you are concerned about, but yourself.

He will be fine, there's no doubt about that. His zest for living, his sense of adventure, his ability to make friends, are all unmatched in your experience. No one does it better. He lives every moment to the fullest, packs every day to the brim with busyness.

But what are you going to do without him? He has been your shadow for the past four years, your helper, your confidant, your little man. How silent, how drained of energy, the house now seems without his constant chatter.

The ringing of the telephone jerks you from your nostalgic melancholy. When you recognize your husband's voice, you ask, "How did it go? Tell me everything. Don't leave out anything."

"It was fairly uneventful until we started down the sidewalk toward the school," he says. "About halfway to the door, he flung himself into my arms and cried, 'Don't leave me, Daddy, don't leave me.'"

"What did you do?"

"What could I do? I carried him to his teacher. It took both of us to unwrap his arms and legs from around me. It was all she could do to hold him as I walked away. I thought my heart would break when he continued to cry, 'Please don't leave me, Daddy, please.' Now I see why you wanted me to take him to school."

"Are you sure he'll be all right?" you ask anxiously.

"His teacher said she would call if he didn't settle down. If you haven't heard from her by this time, I would say he's just fine. In fact, he's probably running the show by now."

Finally, the morning is over, and it is time for you to drive to the school and pick him up. You arrive five minutes early, but you are not alone. A host of other anxious mothers have already gathered to collect their little scholars.

When the bell rings, children pour from the door like ants from a damaged ant hill. Frantically, you strain to catch sight of him, but to no avail. At last you see him, standing in the doorway talking to his teacher.

You honk the car horn, and when he sees you, he comes bounding down the hill with a fist full of papers.

Once in the car, he talks a mile a minute, but you are not listening. With frightening clarity you realize that a chapter in your life is closing. For him it is a beginning, a new adventure, the first step in a journey that will eventually take him into adulthood, away from you, and into a life of his own.

Inside of you, a voice cries, "Don't leave me, Will, please don't leave me." But, being a good mother, you say nothing. Instead, you smile bravely and ask him to tell you again about the little boy whose daddy is a policeman.

3

A Mother's Touch

"A mother's love
is not to be paid back,
but passed on!"

Chapter 3

A Mother's Touch

Above the din of the vacuum cleaner you hear a faint, but familiar sound. You would recognize it anywhere. To anyone else it is just a child's sob, indistinguishable from a thousand others just like it, but you know better. It is her cry, and it is a sound to which you are attuned in your innermost being.

It has been like that from the moment of her birth. It is almost as if the umbilical cord that united the two of you was never severed. What touches her, touches you. Let her stir in her sleep, or even just whimper, and you are instantly awake, no matter how soundly you were sleeping. Though your husband is a doting father who could not love his daughter more, he lacks this primordial instinct. You suppose it is the private domain of mothers.

Now it tears at you, and you rush to the front door and anxiously search the street. You catch sight of her limping toward home, pushing her bike rather than riding it. In an instant you are off the porch, rushing toward her, your heart in your throat.

Between sobs she tells you of racing down the hill at breakneck speed, hitting a patch of gravel and losing control. While she explains, you give her a thorough examination. The palms of both of her hands are badly skinned, and she has a nasty scrape on one knee, but beyond that she seems uninjured.

Once you get her to the house, you kiss the tears on her cheeks and promise to make her an angel food cake as soon as you finish putting a bandage on her knee. The adoring look she gives you takes you back to your own childhood, your youthful misadventures and your mother's healing touch...

How old were you when you cut your hand on the milk bottle? Eight most likely, maybe nine, for you were in the fourth grade. Thinking about it now, you cannot help but smile. How patient your mother was, and how loving. It seemed that her kiss could heal any hurt; could, in fact, right the world's wrongs.

You see it all again, in your mind's eye — the milk bottles sitting in a neat row, against the far wall, on the garage floor. The rain running off the top of the house like a miniature waterfall. One by one you carry the milk bottles and place them where they can catch the rainwater as it pours from the roof. As soon as one is full, you carry it into the garage and replace it with an empty one. In your imagination you are doing important work, and you cannot waste a minute.

Hurrying with a full bottle, you slip on the wet concrete. As if in slow motion you see yourself falling, the bottle shatters on the garage floor and you cut your hand on a jagged piece of broken glass.

Unconsciously, you examine the old scar, still visible after all these years, and your daughter seems to notice it for the very first time.

"Mommy," she asks, "how did you get that scar?"

As you relate the incident, you suddenly remember that your mother hadn't wanted you to play in the rain, but you had begged until she finally relented. How guilty, how irresponsible, she must have felt when you hurt yourself. Still, all you can recall is her tenderness as she tried to stop the bleeding. While the emergency room doctor put the stitches in your hand, she held you in her lap and seemed to suffer at least as much as you did. How precious was the love and comfort she showed you that day.

As you grew older, skinned knees and cut fingers gave way to wounds of the spirit – things like rejection, disappointment and a broken heart. Still, there was no hurt your mother could not heal. Armed with nothing more than her faith in God, and her love for you, she managed to heal every wound you suffered. No matter what came your way, she was there to help you face it.

Although your adolescent difficulties must have seemed inconsequential to her, she never made light of them. She was never too busy, or too tired, to listen as you poured out your pain and frustration. Never did she make you feel foolish by minimizing the seriousness of your concerns. In truth, she had a way of listening that made you feel as if your problems were the most important matters in all the world. And when she prayed for you, you knew everything was going to be all right.

You wonder if your mother knows how much you love her. You hope so, but you are not sure. Once when you tried to tell her, she seemed embarrassed.

"I didn't do anything that you wouldn't do for your daughter," she said, before changing the subject.

With all your heart you wish there were some way you could repay her for all her love and kindness, but try as you might you cannot think of anything.

Suddenly a thought springs into your mind full blown: A mother's love is not to be paid back, but passed on!

Taking your daughter onto your lap, you crush her against your chest. Silently you pray, "God, help me to love my daughter the way my mother loved me..."

After a moment you release her and stand up. Blinking rapidly to clear your tear-blurred vision, you take her by the hand and say, "How about helping me make that angel food cake?"

C H A P T E R

4

The Memory Maker

" Yes, you decide,
making memories is
worth all the effort
it takes."

Chapter 4

The Memory Maker

*T*he house is quiet at last, and you make yourself a cup of tea before sinking wearily into your favorite chair beside the window in the breakfast nook.

You love your parents, your only sister and her family, but having eight extra people in the house for five days is a bit much, not that you would ever complain. It's just that it seems that with that much company on hand at holiday time, all you do is cook and clean. While everyone else is recounting the adventures of childhood, or playing table games, you are in the kitchen making sandwiches or planning dinner. Of course, your mother and sister help, but the responsibility rests squarely on your shoulders.

You wonder, did your mother ever feel this way, all those years when she was playing holiday hostess to a small army of relatives? Probably, but she never let on. With cheerful determination she made every holiday a memorable one. Thinking about it now, you realize how blessed you were, and you breathe a prayer of thanksgiving.

Sipping your tea, you replay the memories of your childhood one more time. You remember a white Christmas in Colorado, a Thanksgiving at your grandparents' farm in Texas, a vacation to Canada and your sixteenth birthday party. How young you were, and how carefree.

Was life really simpler then? you wonder. Probably not. Undoubtedly, it seemed so only because you were a child. For your mother, you are sure it was not easy, seeing that she was familiar with both the pinch of poverty and the pain of tragedy. Yet, you can never remember her indulging in self-pity.

You remember how she bought day-old bread and took in ironing in order to save enough money to give you music lessons. And when she couldn't afford the Easter dress you wanted, she did something better. After studying it at length in the dress shop, she went home and sewed one just like it, only better – hers was stitched with love! How fortunate you were. How fortunate you are.

From her you learned not only how to love your husband and how to make a home, but also the art of making memories for your children. Not five-star productions or expensive extravagances, but ordinary events made somehow special by a mother's loving touch. Like the time she read to you when you were sick, or the time she abandoned her baking to play checkers with you while waiting for your cousins to arrive.

Reliving it now, you recall how time seems to drag, and every few minutes you demand, "How much longer until they get here?" Finally, she wipes her hands on her apron and joins you at the dining room table for a game of checkers. For a few minutes you have her undivided attention, and belatedly you decide that she is more fun than company.

Too soon your cousins arrive, and everyone is talking at once. Your mother and her sister go into the living room to catch up on all the news, while you follow your cousins toward the barn. They live in the city and think the barn is the neatest place in all the world. You know better, but it makes you feel important to show them around, so you pretend that it is as grand as they imagine.

Later, you play hide-and-seek in the creek bottom and swing on the homemade swing. The excitement of soaring over the pond twenty feet below is intoxicating, and they squeal with fearful delight each time it is their turn.

Reluctantly, you make your way toward the house as darkness swallows the last of the day. Rounding the corner, you discover your mother building a fire in the discarded wood stove which now sits in the front yard under the huge oak tree. With her help you roast wieners and marshmallows, and supper becomes a memory rather than just a meal.

Later, around the fire, all of you take turns telling scary stories until it is time for bed.

Initially, such memories may seem inconsequential, fun but not necessarily important. Only when they are seen through the lens of the years does their true value become apparent. In fact, they are tangible proof of your importance, and they affirm your place in the family. As a child, for instance, you simply assumed that your mother loved playing checkers and roasting wieners. Now you know better. It was you she loved!

Tired though you are, you cannot help but smile as you recall how much fun your children have had this Christmas. Although they may not fully appreciate your labor of love, they will someday. Even as time has made your mother's sacrifices obvious to you, so will the passing of the years make yours obvious to them. And years from now, when they are tempted to minimize the importance of family, when they are tempted to choose convenience over tradition, these very memories will challenge them to a higher standard.

Yes, you decide, making memories is worth all the effort it takes. And, in spite of your earlier resolve never to do it again, you begin to make plans for next year. After all, you are the memory maker, the keeper of the family album. It is your investment in the future.

CHAPTER

5

The Imperfect Mom

" 'Lord, Thank you for giving me an imperfect mom, for using her to teach me that love is more important than perfection, that kids are more important than things, and that it is more important to do things with your children rather than just for them.' "

Chapter 5

∞

The Imperfect Mom

It's after ten o'clock, and the children are finally in bed. Your husband is watching the news in the den, and you are curled up on the couch with your Bible and a couple of books. Opening your journal, you read your entry from one year ago today:

"While reading from William Barclay's Daily Study Bible,[1] I discovered a wonderful story about Benjamin West, a British artist of some renown. One day West discovered some bottles of colored ink and to amuse his younger sister Sally he began to paint her portrait. Of course, he made quite a mess, spilling ink here and there. In time his mother discovered him and the mess he had made. Instead of scolding him, she picked up the piece of paper he was working on and exclaimed, 'Why, it's Sally!' Stooping, she kissed him, and Benjamin West says it was her kiss that made him a painter."[1]

---

[1] The Daily Study Bible, "The Letters to the Galatians and Ephesians" by William Barclay

(Edinburgh, Scotland: The Saint Andrew Press, 1962), p. 211.

Tears blur your vision as you read, and you cannot help but think how timely that you should rediscover that beautiful story on this day of all days. You grimace anew as you recall your anger earlier today when you discovered that your seven-year-old had dismantled the antique clock you inherited from your grandmother. Turning back to your journal, you read your prayer from a year ago:

"Lord,

She must have been a remarkable woman,
      wise and perceptive.

Her wisdom makes me feel dull,
      plain.

I'm not nearly so insightful.
Usually I can't see beyond the mess.
Help me, Lord, to be more affirming.
Give me clarity of vision
      that I may discern between budding
            talent and childish irresponsibility.

And if I must err,
      let it be on the side of affirmation
            rather than criticism.

Help me, Lord, for I am just an ordinary woman!"

Your thoughts return to the earlier incident with the clock, and you wonder if your son is a budding mechanical genius or just a curious seven-year-old with a destructive streak. How is a mom to know?

Maybe, you conclude, God is trying to tell you something. Maybe the point of this remarkable coincidence is to remind you that your children are more important than things, even antique clocks. Maybe the Lord is trying to tell you that you need to be more conscientious, more deliberate...

No, you decide, you don't need to be more deliberate. You need to be more spontaneous, more like your mother.

On an impulse you telephone your sister who lives half a continent away. When she answers on the third ring, you plunge right in: "Do you remember the time Mom took us to the police station and had the desk sergeant fingerprint us?"

"How could I forget? We were the envy of all our friends. Their mothers would never do anything like that."

"What about the time she drove nearly two hundred miles just to take us to the circus?"

"That was a hoot, wasn't it?" your sister exclaims. "Especially when we ran out of gas on the way home."

"Mom was one wild and crazy lady," you declare. "No question about that."

"You better believe it," your sister agrees with a chuckle. Turning serious, she adds, "I'm glad she was. If she hadn't taught us to take risks, I don't think I would have ever dared to become a free-lance writer."

You banter memories back and forth for several minutes more, and then your sister asks, "Hey, what prompted all this nostalgia anyway?"

With a sigh you tell her the story about Benjamin West's mother, and then you relate the incident with the antique clock. Before you know it, you are sobbing. "Sometimes I feel like such a failure. I'm afraid I'm going to ruin my kids."

"Don't be silly," she says. "A mistake here and there never ruined anyone. Look at us. We turned out all right, didn't we? And Mom made her share of mistakes, no question about that. Do you remember the time..."

Before long you are laughing hysterically as you take turns recounting your mother's parental blunders. Like everything else she did, they were outrageous. There wasn't a malicious bone in her body, and she would never have done anything to hurt anyone, but she was capable of some scandalous miscalculations. Still, neither you nor your sister seem to have suffered any permanent damage. Maybe there is hope for your children after all.

Finally, you tell your sister good-bye and hang up the telephone, feeling better than you have all day. Returning to your journal, you write:

"Lord,
Thank You for giving me an imperfect mom,
for using her to teach me
that love is more important
than perfection,
that kids are more important
than things,
and that it is more important
to do things
with your children
rather than just for them.

Bless my children, Lord.
Fulfill Your purposes in their lives
in spite of my parental blunders."

Turning out the light, you make your way upstairs toward your bedroom. As you pass the boys' room, you pause. Opening the door quietly, you stand for a moment, lost in the wonder of motherhood. You gave birth to these two sons. They are bone of your bone and flesh of your flesh. Yet they are not really yours, they belong to God. He has simply entrusted you with the privilege of rearing them.

In that moment you decide that your seven-year-old is a mechanical genius. How could you have ever thought otherwise? Brushing his forehead with a kiss, you tiptoe from the room lost in thought as you consider what marvelous things he will invent.

CHAPTER

6

Her First Date

"*Tonight is not 'just' her first date.... It is the beginning of the end, the first domino to fall, and soon the others will follow.*"

Chapter 6

Her First Date

You watch as your daughter puts the final touches on her make-up in preparation for her first date. She is sixteen now, though you cannot imagine how that can be, seeing it was only yesterday that she was an infant nursing at your breast.

How swiftly the years have passed, you think, as fleeting as your first kiss. What you wouldn't give to relive her preschool years, to know again the simple pleasure of giving her a bath before reading her a bedtime story.

Determinedly, you resist the temptation to lose yourself in memories of her childhood. It's not easy, for the past is familiar, safe, not like the present with its gloomy foreshadowing of adulthood.

Grimly, you consider the future. Soon she will be graduating from high school and going off to college. Soon she will meet some handsome guy and fall in love. Soon she will get married and go with her husband to live in some distant city. Soon...

Tonight is not "just" her first date, as your husband so blandly suggests. It is the beginning of the end, the first domino to fall, and soon the others will follow.

It's inevitable, you suppose, and you wouldn't want it any other way, not really. You wouldn't want her to be a wallflower sitting home while all her friends have dates. Still, it would be nice if you could postpone this mad rush toward adulthood just a little longer. You are not ready for it, not yet.

According to your husband, you will never be ready. You suppose he is right. After all, you weren't ready for her to start school, and you weren't ready for her first sleep-over at a friend's house, or her first church camp. With the boys it was easier, but she is your baby, and when she is gone there won't be any more.

She has finished dressing and now poses, waiting for your reaction. Without question she is beautiful, stunning really, and you smile your approval. Her excitement is contagious, and you force yourself to share it. This is not the first time she has gone out with a boy, but always before it was in a group or with adult supervision. This is her first solo date, her first real venture into serious boy-girl things.

For a moment you remember your first date — an awards banquet for the football team. You smile as the memory unfolds. You remember what you wore — an ice-blue dress and your sister's rhinestone necklace. He brought you a corsage, but instead of handing it to you, he tossed it at you. It wasn't the best of beginnings, but as the evening wore on, things got better. By the time he brought you home, you were ready to allow him a single good-night kiss. To your amazement all he did was brush your forehead with his lips before leaving you at the door. At the time you found it rather anti-climatic, but as you think about it now, it seems kind of sweet. Desperately, you hope your daughter's date is equally shy.

The doorbell rings, and for a moment panic seizes you. Looking at your daughter, you see, not the confident young lady she has become, but a vulnerable little girl made even more so by her innocence. She simply cannot imagine the hurts and disappointments life can bring. You want to enfold her in your arms, protect her from all the dangers of living, but you can't. Instead, you kiss her on the cheek and tell her to have a good time.

Watching the taillights disappear down the street, you realize that she is launched and that it will be only a matter of time until she is on her own. There is not much left for you to do, some encouragement and comfort perhaps, but for the most part your job is finished. The person she is destined to be is largely set. Although you cannot protect her from the inherent dangers of life, you pray that you have prepared her for them.

In the end, that is all a mother can do — prepare her children for life. The rest is up to them.

CHAPTER

7

Love on Its Knees

" '... Whether that mother has ever argued out the theory or not, she still prays on. Her intercession is the utterance of her life; it is love on its knees.' "

Chapter 7

∞

Love on Its Knees

It is late, nearly 2:00 A.M., and although your husband has finally succumbed to exhaustion, you cannot sleep. It is two hours past your son's curfew, and your imagination torments you cruelly.

Has he been killed or injured in a terrible auto accident? Is he even now lying in a broken heap along a deserted stretch of rain-slick highway, or being rushed to the nearest trauma center accompanied by the eerie scream of sirens?

Is that a car you hear? Hurrying to the front window, you survey the conspicuously empty driveway and the equally empty street in front of your house. Hope fades, to be replaced by the sick feeling you now identify as fear.

For a long time you stand at the window staring, lost in your tormenting thoughts. Down the street you see a light come on, and you wonder if some other worried mother is waiting for her wayward son or daughter, as you now wait for yours.

It wasn't supposed to be like this, and for a moment you are angry with God. How could He let this happen? You did everything you were supposed to do. You dedicated him to the Lord before he was three weeks old. You read him Bible stories and taught him to say his prayers. You took him to Sunday school and church. So why is this happening?

Your anger fades, to be replaced by guilt. It must be your fault, or your husband's. Maybe you were too strict or not strict enough. Maybe you shouldn't have forced him to attend church when he didn't want to go. Maybe you should have sacrificed to put him in a Christian school rather than sending him to public school. Maybe you should have been more careful with whom you allowed him to associate. Maybe…

At last you fall to your knees, weeping. Unashamedly, you pour out your feelings to God. Desperately you intercede for your son, pleading for his salvation. You implore the Lord to rectify your parental mistakes, to heal whatever damage you may have caused. You acknowledge your help-lessness, throwing yourself on the mercies of God, and little by little your fears give way to faith. God will protect him, of that you are now sure.

Rising from your knees, you make your way to the bookcase and run your finger along the titles until you find Harry Emerson Fosdick's classic, The Meaning of Prayer. Your mother gave it to you a few days before she died. It was one of her favorites, and now you are drawn to it as if by some invisible force.

When you open it, a folded piece of paper flutters to the floor. Picking it up, you discover that it is a note from your mother:

"This book first belonged to my mother, your grandmother, and when she died she passed it on to me. Although it has proved encouraging and inspirational, I never had an occasion to need it in the way my mother did, and I suspect, the way that you will.

"As a young woman I went through a rebellious stage. I rejected everything my parents held sacred. It nearly killed my father, and mother said she would have lost her mind had it not been for this book. When she feared for my very life and eternal soul, she was sustained by the portions about the power of a mother's prayers. Eventually her prayers prevailed, and I returned to the faith of my childhood.

"Why, you may be wondering, am I telling you all of this? Because I see a lot of myself in your Ronnie, and if I am not mistaken he will probably put you through the sort of thing I put my mother through. I hope I am wrong, but I don't think I am. If you ever find yourself fearing for his very soul, I pray that God may use this little book to strengthen you as He used it to strengthen my mother. Her favorite portions are marked. I suggest you begin with the selections on page 183."

With trembling fingers you turn the yellowed pages until you find the desired selections. With tear-blurred eyes you read:

"When a mother prays for her wayward son, no words can make clear the vivid reality of her supplications. Her love pours itself out in insistent demand that her boy must not be lost. She is sure of his value, with which no outward thing is worthy to be compared, and of his possibilities which no sin of his can ever make her doubt. She will not give him up. She follows him through his abandonment down to the gates of death; and if she loses him through death into the mystery beyond, she still prays on in secret, with intercession which she may not dare to utter, that wherever in the moral universe he may be, God will reclaim him. As one considers such an experience of vicarious praying, he sees that it is not merely resignation to the will of God; it is urgent assertion of a great desire. She does not really think that she is persuading God to be good to her son, for the courage of her prayer is due to her certain faith that God also must wish that boy to be recovered from his sin. She rather is taking on her heart the same burden that God has on his; is joining her demand with the divine desire. In this system of personal life which makes up the moral universe, she is taking her place alongside God in an urgent, creative outpouring of sacrificial love.

"Now, this mother does not know and cannot know just what she is accomplishing by her prayers. But we know that such mothers save their sons when all others fail. The mystery of prayer's projectile force is great, but the certainty of such prayer's influence, one way or another, in working redemption for needy lives is greater still. It may be...that God has so ordained the laws of human interrelationship that we can help one another not alone by our deeds but also directly by our thoughts, and that earnest prayer may be the exercise of this power in its highest terms. But whether that mother has ever argued out the theory or not, she still prays on. Her intercession is the utterance of her life; it is love on its knees."[1]

Hugging the open book to your breast, you realize how wise your mother was and how perceptive to have given you this treasure. You embrace the concept, not simply of prayer's redemptive power, but of God's concern for your son. Maybe for the first time you realize that as much as you love Ronnie, God loves him even more.

You remember that your son is not unique, he is not the first boy to wander into the far country.

For instance, Saint Augustine was led into sin, but his sainted mother refused to give up on him. Through her prayers he was eventually brought to a saving knowledge of Jesus Christ, and today he is recognized as one of the early Church Fathers.

Then there's Hudson Taylor, the founder of the Inland China Mission. He was also converted through his mother's persistent prayers, as have been innumerable wayward sons and daughters.

---

[1] Harry Emerson Fosdick, The Meaning of Prayer (New York: Association Press, 1963), p. 183.

Your son will be no exception. His rebellion is no match for your prayers, of that you are sure. It is only a matter of time before he returns to the Faith.

CHAPTER

8

Her Wedding Day

"*It's* over.
Not just the wedding, but
motherhood as you have
known it. You will
always be her mother,
but not in the same way,
not ever again. Your
little girl has given
herself to another."

Chapter 8

Her Wedding Day

She stands beside her father at the head of the aisle, beautiful in her beaded wedding gown, waiting for the organist to begin the wedding march. Her eyes sparkle, you can see that even from your pew at the front of the church, and the smile she gives her father is pure joy. Not even her veil can hide the radiance of her happiness. It emanates from her like heat from a flame.

You share her joy, but yours is bittersweet. Although you are happy for her, you cannot help but note how different things will be once she is married. This will be the first time she has ever lived in a city different from the one in which you live. Who will she confide in when she needs to talk about girl things? Who will she go shopping with on Saturday afternoons? Who will she call when she needs a recipe or advise for getting a spot out?

Suddenly you realize that it is not her you are concerned about, but yourself. She will be busy decorating their apartment and making new friends, but what will you do? The future looms before you as bleak as a boring sermon, and suddenly you are engulfed by an overwhelming sadness. You are not gaining a son, as your husband insists, you are losing your only daughter, your special confidant, your best friend.

For just a moment you hate your future son-in-law. Then the organist booms out the first bars of "Trumpet Voluntary in D Major," and you stand with the rest of the congregation as she begins her journey toward the altar.

Out of the corner of your eye you glimpse your own mother dabbing at the tears now glistening in her eyes. Is she remembering the day you made this same journey? Was her heart torn between joy and sadness as yours is now? Did she wonder, as you are now wondering, if she had done everything she could to prepare you for life and marriage?

Now the bride and her father are at your pew, and you lean forward to receive her embrace. Only it is not a bride you embrace, but a child, an infant, not yet a year old. You place her against your shoulder and gently pat her back in order to burp her. She, in turn, pats your back with her chubby little hand. It is so precious you can't wait to tell your mother.

Once more the present replaces the past, and she now kisses your cheek through her veil. Involuntarily, you compare this sterile kiss with the messy slobbers she gave you as a child. Fiercely, you hug her, as if you could somehow stop the inevitable march of time, could somehow recapture the wonder of those bygone years when you were the most important person in her life.

Then she is gone, and you watch as her father presents her to the groom before joining you on the second pew.

The minister begins the ceremony, and you study the bride and groom intently. They make a handsome couple, anyone can see that. Brent — tall, blond, handsome. Crystal — pretty, dark-haired, radiant. Two young lovers smiling fearlessly, confident that their love can conquer anything life may bring.

Glancing at your husband, you wonder, were we ever that idealistic? You suppose so, but now you are more practical, more realistic, and you cannot help but be concerned.

Brent is ambitious, and he has a good position with a growing company, so he should be able to provide for Crystal. But, you wonder, will he be able to give both his marriage and his career the attention they need? Crystal is a loving person who requires lots of affection. Without it, she will shrivel up and die like a flower without water.

You are a lot like that yourself. Well do you remember the early, difficult days of your own marriage. Once when your husband's work required him to be away from home several days at a time, you fell into a deep depression. In desperation you called your father and told him you were coming home. Kindly, he replied, "You are home." You worked things out, but it wasn't easy, and you would hate to see Crystal go through anything like that.

Brent sounds so sincere as he vows to love and cherish her his whole life long. You do not doubt his sincerity, but neither are you naive enough to believe that he has any real comprehension of what he is promising. Will he truly love and care for her if she develops a chronic illness, or for that matter, will he love her if she loses her girlish figure after giving birth to two or three children? What you really want to know is, will he love her as much as you do?

The minister pronounces them husband and wife, and the rest of evening passes in a blur of activities. Too soon the newlyweds depart beneath a deluge of rice and best wishes to begin their new life together.

As the taillights of the rented limo disappear around the corner, a melancholy tiredness settles upon you. It's over. Not just the wedding, but motherhood as you have known it. You will always be her mother, but not in the same way, not ever again. Your little girl has given herself to another.

Taking your husband's hand, you walk side by side without speaking, each of you lost in thought. Being a mother is the most rewarding, the most fulfilling experience in life, of that you are sure. As you consider all the love you have given your children, the sacrifices you have made for them, you decide that maybe the most loving thing a mother can do is to love them enough to let them go.

Never have you felt so vulnerable. Crystal's happiness is more important to you than your own. Yet, you are powerless, for the most part, to determine whether she will be happy or not. No longer can you protect her from the cruel world or from the consequences of her own irresponsible choices. Not that you ever could, really, but you managed to maintain that illusion as long as she lived at home.

Remembering that you were young and foolish not so many years ago gives you some comfort. Still, you can't help remembering the dumb things you did and the way you suffered for your mistakes. The fact that God redeemed your most painful experiences, made even your most irresponsible choices somehow contribute to His ultimate plan for your life, encourages you, but it doesn't make you feel any less vulnerable.

If you could, you would protect Brent and Crystal from life, from the very things God uses to make us truly His people. In truth, you are thankful that you can't, but you still fear for them.

You wish there were some way to become wise without the pain of experience. There isn't, so you simply commit them to the Lord praying, "Redeem their inexperience, O Lord, and mine too for that matter, for we are indeed people in need of Your wisdom and grace."

In the end that is all a mother can do. Ultimately, the care and protection of her children rests in the hands of their loving heavenly Father.

Other books by Richard Exley
are available at your local bookstore.

Straight From the Heart for Dad

Straight From the Heart for Couples

Straight From the Heart for Graduates

How to Be a Man of Character
In a World of Compromise

Marriage in the Making

The Making of a Man

Abortion

Blue-Collar Christianity

Life's Bottom Line

Perils of Power

The Rhythm of Life

When You Lose Someone You Love

The Other God —
Seeing God as He Really Is

The Painted Parable

HB
HONOR
BOOKS

Tulsa, Oklahoma

To contact the author, write:

Richard Exley
P.O. Box 54744
Tulsa, Oklahoma 74155

Please include your prayer requests
when you write.